The Substance of Things

by
Charles Capps

The Substance
of Things

by
Charles Capps

Harrison House
Tulsa, Oklahoma

6th Printing
Over 36,000 in Print

The Substance of Things
ISBN 0-89274-599-1
Copyright © 1990 by Charles Capps
P. O. Box 69
England, Arkansas 72046

Published by Harrison House, Inc.
P. O. Box 35035
Tulsa, Oklahoma 74153

Contents

Preface

In this book I refer to the heart and human spirit many times. I use them interchangeably for the purpose of making it simple to understand.

I realize that in Scripture they are not always the same, and I don't mean to imply that in every case they are the same. But in the context of this book, I am convinced that what the Bible calls the heart and the human spirit bring about the same purpose — that is to receive, produce or lead us to all that is needed to bring fulfillment of the promises of God in our lives.

1

The Word Created

In the beginning was the Word, and the Word was with God, and the Word was God.

All things were made by him; and without him was not any thing made that was made.

John 1:1,3

All things were made by him . . . . Him Who? Him, the Word.

Without Him was not any thing made that was made. Nothing was made without the Word. The verses above are talking about Jesus, Who is the Word of God personified.

And he (Jesus) is before all things, and by him all things consist.

Colossians 1:17

Everything was created by Him — (the Word) — and by the Word all things consist.

> **Through faith we understand that the worlds were framed by the word of God, so that things which are seen were not made of things which do appear.**
>
> Hebrews 11:3

In other words, we understand it was through faith that the worlds were framed by God's Word. Whether you realize it or not, you frame your world with your words daily. Whether you're speaking words filled with faith or fear, you're framing your world, and you will live in it.

Words transmit. They will transmit faith or fear. If you always talked about bad news, that transmits oppression and fear. If you talked about good news, that would transmit faith. Words produce after their kind.

The gospel is the Good News. Jesus said:

> **The thief cometh not, but for to steal, and to kill, and to destroy: I am come that they might have life, and that they might have it more abundantly.**
>
> John 10:10

Jesus said, **I am come**. Thank God He has come. The Word has come that you might have life and that you might have it more abundantly. The Good News of the Word creates an abundant life for spirit, soul and body. Speaking God's words creates faith, and faith is the substance of things God has given us.

Words Create Images

If you continue to give voice to God's Word, if you continue to proclaim God's promises, they will create an image inside you. If you proclaim what the devil says, you'll have an image created by the devil's words. Images are created and perfected by words.

For instance, if you had never seen my automobile, I could describe it to you in such detail that you would have an image inside you of what it looks like. You could go find it and say, "I know that is his car." How would you know if you had never seen it? Oh, but you did see it — just as I described it, because my words produced an image inside you.

Your mind creates powerful images out of words you hear. Words can even make you recall images that you have seen before. For instance, let me walk you around your house with words.

We will start at the front of your house. Look at the shrubs you have been intending to trim. You can see the front door needs painting. You can see the loose shingles that you've been intending to fix. You can walk all around your house and see it in your spirit. Why didn't you see a birthday cake? Because my words controlled what you saw.

Words produce images. They also recall and change images. Use the right kinds of words and you will create the right kinds of images. When the Word of God gets in you, it creates an image after its kind. When that image is perfected inside you, then faith has come.

Faith Comes by Hearing

Paul says, **God hath dealt to every man the measure of faith** (Rom. 12:3). What is the measure of faith? How do you measure faith? You measure faith by the amount of God's Word that abides in you.

Faith is in the Word. That is why faith cometh by hearing the Word; the Word controls the image you have inside. So the only way you can measure faith is to measure the amount of Word that is in you.

The measure is the faith that is in the Bible — that is the total measure. God has dealt that faith to every man, but not all men have faith because not all will receive the Word. But that is all the Bible faith there is, and God has given it to all who will receive it.

The process is started by hearing the Word of God. Faith is measured by the amount of Word you conceive in your heart.

2

God's Provision Through Faith

For he (Jesus) hath made him to be sin for us, who knew no sin; that we might be made the righteousness of God in him.

2 Corinthians 5:21

God has made provision, abundant provisions, for his people. He has provided salvation by the blood of Jesus for your healing by the stripes that were on his back. Jesus said:

I am come that they might have life, and that they might have it more abundantly.

John 10:10

The way you enter into those provisions is through faith. That faith comes from the Word. Paul put it this way:

> **So then faith cometh by hearing, and hearing by the word of God.**
>
> Romans 10:17

Rightstanding with God comes only through faith.

The law of the Old Covenant was works. The law of the New Covenant is faith.

Under the Old Covenant there was a limited righteousness, and it came through works. Under the New Covenant we are under grace. The only way you can enter into grace is through faith. (Eph. 2:8; Rom. 5:1,2.) It's through faith, not works, that you enter into a place of rightstanding with God.

We become the righteousness of God. (2 Cor. 5:21.) It is not our own righteousness, but His righteousness that has been imputed to us.

Receiving What God Has Already Given

God has given to us all things that pertain to life and godliness. But we must act on His Word to possess what has already been given. Second Peter 1:3 says:

According as his divine power hath given unto us all things that pertain unto life and godliness, through the knowledge of him that hath called us to glory and virtue.

God has already given. It isn't a matter of praying long enough for God to give it to us — it's a matter of receiving what God has already given us. The conception must take place in the human spirit.

Someone said it this way: It must be conceived in the womb of the spirit, then it will be manifested outwardly. Salvation, baptism of the Holy Spirit, divine healing — whatever it is you receive from God — must be received first into the heart which I will refer to as the human spirit. (Mark 11:24, Rom. 10:10.)

Faith works in the heart. Paul says:

For with the heart man believeth unto righteousness.

Romans 10:10

You can't believe with your head the things you can believe with the heart. You can give mental assent, but faith works in the heart.

Romans 10:8 says: **But what saith it? The word is nigh thee, even in thy mouth, and in thy heart: that is, the word of faith, which we preach.** The way you get faith into your heart is by hearing yourself speak God's Word. Faith in God and faith for the provision God has made for you comes from hearing the Word of God.

There is a reciprocal to that truth, and knowing it is vital. If faith in God comes by hearing God's Word, then faith in the devil comes by hearing the words of the devil.

You would be surprised at the number of people who say to me that the devil told them such and such and ask if I have a word from the Lord for them.

I say, "Yes, I have a word for you. Quit listening to and quoting the devil!" Faith comes by hearing whether it's God or the devil you're hearing.

Once you have quoted and spoken the promises of God until faith is abundantly in your heart, then because of faith you speak words that cause the manifestation of the things promised.

God gives us an example in the first chapter of Genesis. He spoke things into existence. In the beginning God looked out and saw darkness over the face of the deep, and the Spirit of God moved upon the face of the waters. (Gen. 1:2.) Even though the Holy Ghost was there, no change took place until God said, **Let there be light.**

God saw darkness, but He didn't talk about darkness. He called for light. God filled His words with faith to cause the things He said to come into manifestation. There was an image inside Him. He expressed it in words. The image you have inside you will also be expressed in words. Those words set the cornerstones of your life.

3

Beyond Faith

Now faith is the substance of things hoped for, the evidence of things not seen.

Hebrews 11:1

What is it we hope for? I don't know about you, but I hope for what God has given me, and 2 Peter 1:3 says He has given me all things that pertain to life and godliness. How?

Through the knowledge of him that hath called us to glory and virtue.

2 Peter 1:3

If you don't have knowledge of it, you couldn't have faith for it. Faith is the substance, and it is the evidence of things not seen.

Sometimes I think we are guilty of putting so much emphasis on faith that people get hung up on faith alone when we need to go on beyond faith.

We can teach only as much as we've received. But God continually reveals more about His Word as we continue in it. What we know now is true, but we'll know even more as we continue to study His Word.

Hebrews 11:1 says, **...faith is the substance of things hoped for, the evidence of things not seen.** Why is it not seen? Because we don't have enough light on the subject to project the correct image. If you can't see some things, it's because you don't have enough light on it or it's too far away when actually they are here for us now.

The Words Give Light

David said, **The entrance of thy words giveth light** (Ps. 119:130).

The more Word you have on any one subject, the more light you will have. Faith is the substance of things. One translation says the "title-deed." It's the substance of things hoped for, the evidence of what you can't see.

If you had never heard the scripture that says Jesus bore our sicknesses and our diseases (Is. 53:4), He bore our sins with His own body on the tree that we being dead in sin should live under righteousness and that by His stripes ye were healed (1 Pet. 2:24) — if somebody told you these things, you might say, "I'll have to go by faith on that, because I haven't read it or experienced it.

"I don't know whether that's right or not as far as experiencing it, but if it's the Word of God, I'll take it by faith, and I'll release my faith in the Word of God."

You know what you're doing? You're laying hold by faith on the promise until the manifestation. By faith, you're saying it. By faith, you're confessing it. That means you have no outward evidence.

But as you study the Word, you find that Jesus said:

> **What things soever ye desire, when ye pray, believe that ye receive them, and ye shall have them.**
>
> Mark 11:24

As you go on studying and confessing the Word, you get that same image inside you, and one day it becomes alive to you and you say, "Hey, it's already been provided. It's really mine!" You read in Second Peter 1:3,4:

> **According as his divine power hath given unto us all things that pertain unto life and godliness, through the knowledge of him that hath called us to glory and virtue:**
>
> **Whereby are given unto us exceeding great and precious promises: that by these ye might be partakers of the divine nature, having escaped the corruption that is in the world through lust.**

You think, "It's already given! He's already done it."

Move Into a Realm of Knowledge

You're gaining knowledge of Him, and all things that pertain unto life and godliness are given through this knowledge of Him — knowing what He said and knowing He has done it. This is the knowledge that taps God's provisions. This is knowledge revealed by the Spirit of God's Word. Second Peter 1:5 states:

> **And beside this, giving all diligence, add to your faith virtue; and to virtue knowledge.**

In other words don't stop at faith. Go on to knowledge. Then act on what you know.

Years ago when I gave an offering, it took all the faith I had to believe that God would multiply that which I planted. But it is not that way now. Because now I have too much knowledge to doubt. I know God will multiply that which I plant.

I'm just acting on what I know — I don't have to be actively concerned about faith, although faith is there. I have by faith moved over into a realm of knowledge. Now I'm operating in what I know, not on just what I believe. When the faith image is perfected in us, we should move and act because of what we know.

You have too much knowledge to doubt that you can get in your car and drive it. (Unless you're four payments behind! Then you might doubt it!) You don't have to actively use your faith to get in your car and drive it — you have too much knowledge to doubt that.

The Law was a school master to bring people to Christ. It was the school master to bring you to a better covenant. But after faith has come, you're no longer under the school master.

Under the New Covenant, I believe that faith is your school master to bring the image of the promise into focus. Then when the image is perfected in you (in your spirit), you've moved to a higher plane. Now you know beyond any doubt. You're no longer struggling in that area of faith. Even though faith is there, the struggle is over and you know.

Don't misunderstand what I'm saying. I'm not saying that you don't need faith. Faith is there all right, but you've moved up a notch higher. You've moved up to the level where faith and knowledge have been fused together in your spirit. The matter is then a settled issue and you just act on what you know.

Sometimes you hear people say, "You never know what God will do." You will if you read His Word. *If you know what God will do, He'll do it. If you don't know what God will do, He's under no obligation.*

Faith brings you into this knowledge. And when you know that you know, there's no struggle with faith. **. . . faith is the substance of things hoped for, the evidence of things not seen.**

Once you see it clearly in your spirit, then you know and act.

4

The Invisible Things of God

**For the invisible things of him from
the creation of the world are clearly seen,
being understood by the things that are
made, even his eternal power and Godhead; so that they are without excuse.**

Romans 1:20

The verse above when in context makes the point of the passage, but this verse alone also gives us a general principle.

The way to understand the invisible things of God, even the eternal power in the Godhead, is to look at the things that are made. The Godhead can be understood by understanding the man that God created. God created man in His image, in His likeness. (Gen. 1:26.)

God is a Spirit (John 4:24). The Godhead consists of the Father, the Son and the Holy Ghost. Man was created a spirit being and in so much exact duplication of God's kind that he is a three-fold being which consists of spirit, soul and body.

God's Spirit bears witness with our spirit. (Rom. 8:16.) Jesus was the physical manifestation of God upon this earth — He relates to the physical man. He always called Himself the Son of man. The soul of man is composed of his will, his mind and his emotions. That's essentially his guidance system, and the Holy Spirit is called our Teacher and Guide. (John 14:26, 16:13.) So there you have an example of the invisible things of God revealed by understanding the man God made.

God, Who is a spirit, created this world and everything in it. The laws that govern the spirit world have been extended into this earth.

So to understand the things of God in that invisible world, we must examine the things God made. They give us clear understanding of the invisible things of God.

Parables of Jesus

The parables of Jesus reveal the invisible things of God. That is why Jesus in parables talked about shepherds, sheepfolds, and sowing and reaping. The parable of the sower in Mark 4:3-9 is the greatest of all the parables of the Kingdom of God. Notice verse 13: **And he** (Jesus) **said unto them, Know ye not this parable? and how then will ye know all parables?** In other words, "If you don't understand this parable, how will you understand all parables of the Kingdom?"

God's Word Is the Seed

Jesus said, **the sower soweth the word** (v. 14). He tells you that the Word of God is the seed (Luke 8:11) the ground where you sow it is the heart of man. (Mark 4:15.)

Let's look at some of these things Jesus said.

If ye have faith as a grain of mustard seed, ye shall say unto this mountain, Remove hence to yonder place; and it

shall remove; and nothing shall be impossible unto you.

Matthew 17:20

If ye have faith . . . *ye shall say* . . . . By saying, you sow the seed in the heart.

Mark 4:26-28 says:

> So is the kingdom of God, as if a man should cast *seed into the ground;*

> And should sleep, and rise night and day, and the seed should spring and grow up, he knoweth not how.

> For the earth bringeth forth fruit of herself; first the blade, then the ear, after that the full corn in the ear.

When you cast seed into the ground, you go to bed and get up, and the seed springs and grows without you knowing how. Jesus is telling us exactly how to sow a seed in the realm of the spirit. He's telling us how the spirit world of the Kingdom of God works, revealing it to us through the things that are made.

One of "the things that was made," was the earth, and it will produce. But you must plant a seed. The Bible tells us that the Word of God is the incorruptible seed. (1 Pet. 1:23.)

The Seed Determines Production

The earth is under a curse. (Gen. 3:17.) Generally speaking, if you are going to raise anything on this planet earth that's good, you have to force the earth to produce it.

Have you noticed you don't have to plant the curses? They're already out there. Just leave your garden alone and the curses will come up — weeds, crab grass, and Johnson grass.

But to produce anything good, you must force the earth to produce it. This is what I call the dominion principle. You have to take dominion over the soil. How? With the seed.

You can force the soil to produce. The seed makes a demand on the soil. The soil has no choice about the matter — once the seed is properly planted, it has to respond to that seed. The soil doesn't decide what to produce. *The seed is the dominion factor.* The seed determines what will be produced.

The law of Genesis (1:11,12) says that everything produces after its kind — every grass, every fruit tree whose seed is in itself. The ability to produce is in the seed itself.

God's Word has a live germ in it, and that seed will produce exactly after its kind. That seed is planted by saying.

Mark 11:23 says, **That whosoever shall say. . . . and shall not doubt in his heart, but shall believe that those things which he saith shall come to pass; he shall have whatsoever he saith.**

What will he have? He shall have whatsoever he saith. We could say it this way: "He shall have whatsoever he soweth."

As we understand the laws that govern this world and work in agreement with them, then we can reap the harvest God has provided in the spirit world through *his promises which are seeds of blessings.*

The blessing is contained in the seed and will be manifest after it is planted. If you had faith as a seed, you should say what you believe.

5

The Seed
Is in Itself

The ability to reproduce the promise from the Word of God in your life is in the promise itself.

If you look closely at a photograph in the newspaper, you will see that it is made up of a series of dots. (You can see this clearly with a magnifying glass.) In fact, essentially that's what printed matter is — a series of dots. The picture is made up of dots shaded different colors. The substance of that photograph is a series of dots.

Let's say there are 2,000 dots in a photograph. That same number of dots can be a photograph of a child playing or a photograph of a train wreck. It's the same number of dots, but they are rearranged to create a different image.

God's Word says that faith is the substance of things. Let's call *faith the dots that make up the substance of things.*

If you know what the Bible says about certain subjects and you speak the opposite, you're rearranging the dots! For example, I know that from Luke 6:38 if I give, it will be given to me.

But what if I give, and my washing machine breaks down? Then the car doesn't start, and I have to buy a new battery for my car? Then I am tempted to rearrange the dots to conform to what I experience by saying: "That's the way it happens every time — I give, and everything I have starts breaking down!" What am I doing? If I do that, I'm rearranging the dots! But we should say it the way God said it. Don't tamper with the dots!

Speak the Word

Remember that the same dots that created a picture of a child playing can also produce a picture of a tragedy. So don't rearrange the dots. *God's Word is preprogrammed.* The seed is in itself. The ability to reproduce a promise in God's Word is in the promise itself. *Don't rearrange* the substance (dots).

If you give, and your washing machine and car both break down, stay with the Word. Let it abide in you by saying, "I have given; and *it is given* unto me good measure, pressed down, and shaken together, and running over, men give into my bosom. For with the same measure that I give, it shall be given to me."

In other words let God's Word abide in you, regardless of present circumstances. Don't rearrange the dots to conform to what you experienced, but rather let your confession establish the dots the way God arranged them. Then you will change what you experience.

Have you ever watched a child fill in one of those sheets of paper with a bunch of dots that are all numbered? If the child draws lines that follow the numbers in sequence between 1, 2, 3, 4 and so forth, he draws a perfect image. But if he zigzags across the page out of sequence from 1 to 7 to 3 to 9, he will have a confused mess, because he changed the image that was preprogrammed by the numbers and the data.

God's Word is preprogrammed. The seed is in itself. The ability to produce exactly what was promised is preprogrammed into that Word. If you connect the dots in the way it was intended, if you speak God's words in the way God intended, you'll create the right image and in the days to come, you will live it out in reality.

6

God Is Never Late

The more you confess the Word, the better that image will be perfected in you. When you first start saying that your need is met, you'll think, "I'm just lying. I don't have abundance." But God said if you give, it will be given unto you. (Luke 6:38.) He said if you sow bountifully, you'll reap bountifully. (2 Cor. 9:6.)

If you keep speaking God's words long enough, you'll get the dots lined up inside you, you'll see the promise as being fulfilled, then you'll live out the reality of it in your life.

In photography whatever you expose film to is the image that will be formed on that film. The human spirit is like film in a camera. Whatever you continually expose it to is the image that will be formed in it.

For example, you could walk a two-by-four if it were on the floor with no problem. But what if we raised that same two-by-four 20 feet high? Most people couldn't walk it. Why? Because they could see themselves falling.

Would you walk that two-by-four if it were stretched across the Grand Canyon? Now remember, it's the same two-by-four — not any smaller than it was when it was on the floor — but the consequences of falling are greater.

When I say, "Can you walk a two-by-four?" you say, "Yes," because you can see yourself doing it. But when I say, "Across the Grand Canyon?" you say, "No," because you now see yourself falling. The height caused you to rearrange the dots. Now you have a different image.

Whatever you expose your spirit to is the image that will be formed in you. Then eventually you will live out the reality of that image. That's why Paul said, **The word is nigh thee, even in thy mouth, and in thy heart** (Rom. 10:8).

Notice it's in *your mouth and then in your heart*. You talk defeat, and you will be defeated. You defeat yourself by your own words. God's Word is preprogrammed. It will put you over in life. It will produce the results that God promised, but it won't happen overnight, so don't get in a hurry. When you get in a hurry, you miss God's best.

I'm going to put in my coon-dog story to make this next point clear. There was a guy who was bragging about having the best coon dog in the country.

"He's the fastest thing on a coon you ever saw. And one thing about this dog, he never lies. When he trees, you'll get a coon."

His friend said, "I want to see that dog hunt."

So they went hunting and, sure enough, that dog treed a coon in ten minutes. But after a while the dog treed up a little sapling that didn't have a leaf on it.

The sapling was 20 feet high, not a hole in it, and there was no coon to be found in that tree.

The friend said, "I thought you said this dog didn't lie."

The guy said, "Well, I forgot to tell you one thing. Not very often but once in a while this dog is so fast that sometimes he gets here before the coon does. Just sit down. That coon will be along any minute!"

Sometimes we don't plant the seed early enough for the harvest to come up by the time we need it.

If your house payment is due January 1, don't start December 29 confessing that you have abundance. Start confessing a year before the payment is due. Let the Word build that image of abundance inside you.

God's never late, but many times we expect our harvest too early. There are some people who are looking for their harvest and haven't planted anything. There is no harvest without planting. So plant it, and give it time. God does not lie. God's Word works.

7

Calling Those Things Which Be Not as Though They Were

If your pastor gets up in front of you, holds up a piece of paper and says, "This is our new church," you're not going to accuse him of lying are you? But that piece of paper isn't the church — it's a blueprint, an image.

Romans 4:17 tells us that God **calleth those things which be not as though they were.** The pastor calls the blueprint a church when it isn't a church. It's only an image on paper. But he says, "Here's our new church."

What did that church start with? It started with words: Someone said, "We ought to build a new church. How big

will we build it?" Then some figures
were put down on paper. Words. **In the
beginning was the Word** (John 1:1) —
Jesus.

Your Miracle Begins
With Words

Your miracle always begins with God's
Word. It starts with God's words being
imprinted in your heart.

Don't lend your voice to the enemy,
because he will put an image inside you
with your own words that will destroy
what God has given you. If you'll say
what God says about you, you'll end up
with a blueprint, and if you follow that
blueprint, the rest will come together.

Allow me to use another example.

The image on your TV screen is made
up of a series of lines made up of a series
of dots. There are about 2,000 of the lines
across that TV screen, and they're all
made up of dots. There are about 750,000
dots that make up that image on the TV.
Those dots are the sum total of the
substance of the picture on that screen.

The camera is used to transfer the image. The TV set receives different colors and shades which rearrange the image on the screen. It's the same number of dots, but they make up a different image. On a TV screen, the substance of the image is in the dots.

Faith is the substance of things. God's Word is preprogrammed to produce what is promised. The substance of things is faith. The dots (faith) are preprogrammed into God's Word. If you don't rearrange the dots, the image will always come out the same as the Word. To perfect that image, you must speak, proclaim — say — what God said in His Word. Eventually that image will be formed inside you.

That's what it means to speak the word of faith. You speak God's Word and faith comes as a result of your speaking, because the Word is filled with faith.

If you're hurting and sick, confess, "By His stripes I was healed!" Don't change the dots. That's the way God said it.

First Peter 2:24 says:

Who his own self bare our sins in his own body on the tree, that we, being dead to sins, should live unto righteousness: by whose stripes ye were healed.

Notice it doesn't say you were going to be healed, it says you were healed.

If you say, "I believe God's going to do it sometime," He won't. You're rearranging the dots.

In the realm of the spirit, it's already happened. Focus God's words into your spirit. When you get that image in your spirit, then you'll live in the reality of it. The problem is that too many people are rearranging the dots, and it never comes into focus.

Don't Give Up

I believe the Word of God produces an image in you much the same way that a Polaroid camera produces a photo. The Polaroid material works by the polarization of light.

The film is light sensitive after it is exposed. As the film slides out of the camera, rollers spread a chemical over the film which starts the developing process. The image is already implanted on the film, but cannot be seen until the developing process is complete. The film is so sensitive that it will imprint exactly the image you saw in the viewfinder.

When you say, "Thank God I have abundance and no lack; I have given and it's given unto me: good measure, pressed down, and shaken together, and running over," you expose your film (spirit) to the promise of God. Even though there is no immediate manifestation, the process has begun.

Remember, **The entrance of thy Words giveth light** (Ps. 119:130). The light of God's Word will polarize your spirit, but it takes time for the process to be completed. But if you say, "That's what I figured — I've tried for three days, and it didn't work," that is like snapping your Polaroid camera and catching the film when it slides out, then throwing it away saying the camera doesn't work because you can't see the photo immediately.

But go back after a while and pick it up. You'll see what you threw away. That light sensitive film was exposed, and the chemical has had its effect on it. Just wait a few minutes, and that photograph will develop right before your eyes.

If you didn't understand how a polaroid camera works, you might pull the film out of the camera, and say, "There's nothing here!" You would throw it down and say, "This camera doesn't work!" There appears to be nothing on the film. But if you'll give it time, it will develop right before your eyes.

8

Ears To Hear
so You Can See

You have two sets of ears, not just two ears. You have the outer ear and the inner ear. I believe the inner ear is designed by God to send what you speak directly into your heart (spirit). Have you noticed when you plug up your ears and talk, your voice sounds louder to you?

Let's liken the human spirit to film in a Polaroid camera. You expose it with *your voice.* Expose the film by speaking God's Word; then don't give up before the manifestation comes. So be careful what you give voice to, for it makes a lasting impression on your spirit.

Ephesians 4:29 says:

> **Let no corrupt communication proceed out of your mouth, but that which**

**is good to the use of edifying, that it
may minister grace unto the hearers.**

You should let the things that you say
give grace to the hearer. Who is the
number one hearer of what you say? *You
are.*

Have you ever heard your voice on a
tape recorder? Did you say, "That
sounds just like me, doesn't it?" No.
You were probably embarrassed and said,
"Oh, no, that couldn't be me!" But that's
the way everyone else has been hearing
you all the time.

You sounded different to yourself,
because you had never heard yourself
totally with the outer ear until you heard
yourself on tape. You pick up much of
your voice through the inner ear.

Paul said: ...**The word is nigh thee,
even in thy mouth, and in thy heart: that
is, the word of faith, which we preach**
(Rom. 10:8). The Word of God is in your
mouth then in your heart.

Notice that the Word gets in your
mouth first. You can learn about the
Word. You can hear about the Word.
But until you speak it, it has not reached
its highest form. Remember Jesus said,

It is the spirit that quickeneth; the flesh profiteth nothing: the *words* that I speak unto you, they are spirit, and they are life (John 6:63). The words you speak — if they are words of life — give life, quicken, make alive. But the words of the devil bring death, destruction and evil.

> **Death and life are in the power of the tongue: and they that love it shall eat the fruit thereof.**
>
> Proverbs 18:21

God designed us so that the words we speak go directly into our hearts. The intent was to give life, make alive, quicken the human spirit within.

Remember Jesus said:

> **If ye had faith as a grain of mustard seed, ye might say unto this sycamine tree, Be thou plucked up by the root, and be thou planted in the sea; and it should obey you.**
>
> Luke 17:6

You would sow the seed by saying what you believe. You expose the film of your human spirit with your voice. Your voice of faith creates an image of the promise being fulfilled in your life. You will then be able to see yourself living out the reality of that promise months before you physically have the manifestation of it in your life.   But the Word you heard through your voice caused you to see it before it actually happened.

9

God's Word Reproduces

How a Copy Machine Works

Here is essentially how some copy machines work. The paper which goes through the copier is negatively charged. When you make a photocopy, you put the original on the glass and punch the button. The bright light comes on and exposes the negatively charged paper which causes all areas except the shaded image to lose its negative charge.

Only the image has an electrical charge and when exposed to the carbon particles which have a positive charge, it attracts the carbon to the image only. That is the only place it will stick.

This is what happens when the entrance of God's Word brings light to you. It eliminates the negative charge in you except where it agrees with the original word of promise. Then you draw the blessings promised.

If you were able to pull that sheet of exposed paper out of the copier before it is exposed to the carbon particles, you would say, "There's nothing on this paper!" because you couldn't see it. But an electrical charge is there that will draw the carbon needed to produce the exact image of the original.

Let's say it this way — when you confess the promise from God's Word, you expose your copy paper (your heart or spirit). But much like the Polaroid film, you have to give the image time to develop. Keep it up until you have a clear image of the word inside you. The charge becomes established in you, and then as you go through life you will draw all that is needed to live out the exact image of the original promise. That's why you don't have to proofread the copy. The exact image transferred from the original promise to your life.

That's the way God's Word produces in you. God's Word is preprogrammed if it is spoken in faith. The very image is transferred to you. The entrance of the Word into your spirit releases light that perfects the image. Then you will attract all that is necessary to live out the reality of the Word.

10

The Seed
Will Never Fail

Being born again, not of corruptible seed, but of incorruptible, by the word of God, which liveth and abideth for ever.

1 Peter 1:23

God's Word is incorruptible seed. That seed will never fail. But what you do or don't do with the seed can cause a production failure. If you start rearranging the dots (Word), you're going to alter the outcome.

If you say, "But here's the way I believe — I believe that God heals sometimes, but sometimes God makes you sick," you're rearranging the dots and creating a different image than what the Word portrayed. You will attract the curses rather than the blessings.

Jesus said, . . . **the words that I speak
unto you, they are spirit, and they are life**
(John 6:63).   God's Words charge the
human spirit so that when you even get
close to a blessing, it will stick to you.

When you are charged up with God's
Word, you can walk right out in the midst
of the curses, and the curses will run off
you like water off a duck's back.   They
will not stick in the same way that carbon
will not stick to paper unless it is charged.

Attract the Blessings, not the Curses!

There's another side to this: If you
begin to say what the devil said, you can
charge the human spirit so that you
attract the curses instead of the blessings.

Don't ever say things like: "I always
get the flu this time of the year — I'm
always the first one to get it." "If I ever
get a good job I'll lose it.   You watch and
see — I'll be the first one laid off down
at the plant."

If you confess those things, you can
walk in the middle of blessings, and they
will be repelled — but the curses will
stick.   With such negative talk, you'll

draw the curses like a magnet draws metal. But if you are charged with faith, you'll attract the promises of God in your life.

(When Brother Capps was teaching this message, he went into the prophecy below.)

For the life that is in My Word will draw from my provisions all that has been determined by the measure of which your spirit has been exposed to My Word.

That anointing shall flow and the power of God shall know the exactness of the moment in time where it shall come and where you should be. Then you will see that all that you proclaim shall surely be as you walk in the light of all that's revealed.

You'll draw from my provisions. You'll walk in a day when they say it can't be. But it will be, because you have given yourself to know my will and my purpose — my anointing shall fulfill the desire that my Word creates within you.

The desire that is created by My Word. I will always fulfill, and

it'll surely come to pass for My
Word is out, and I will perform it.

11
Mingled Seed

Ye shall keep my statutes. Thou shalt not let thy cattle gender with a diverse kind: thou shalt not sow thy field with mingled seed: neither shall a garment mingled of linen and woollen come upon thee.

Leviticus 19:19

Mingled seed can't produce after its own kind. God instructed Israel not to sow mingled seed.

Don't Tamper With the Seed

Many people sow mingled seed. If you say, "I know sometimes God will heal us, but sometimes He makes us sick," you're sowing mingled seed.

I believe a mingled seed is what we call today a hybrid. I call it a lowbrid.

It isn't either this one or that one — it's a cross between the two.

The religious systems have done this for years: they've mingled man's ideas with the truth to the point that it won't produce anything.   A hybrid won't produce after its kind.   But God's Word always produces after its kind.

A mule is a hybrid — it is a cross between a donkey and a horse — but it can't reproduce.   Man tampered with God's creation.   (Have you heard the expression "stubborn as a mule"?)

The Bible tells us not to mingle seed. It won't produce after its kind.   You can't plant the seed from a hybrid plant the next year and expect to have a hybrid plant, because the seed will revert back to a lower form.

When you plant mingled seed in your life, it will always revert back to the lower form, the curses.   Poverty and sickness are usually the results.

Be careful that you don't tamper with the seed.   Say it the way God said it. When you say what God said and at other times say what the devil said, you're mingling the seed.   You'll confuse your heart. (James 1:26.) But if you'll go with God's original Word, you'll get a harvest of the same kind, a copy of the original. Then you don't have to proofread the copy.

Remember all the other examples: Don't tamper with the dots. The dots are the substance of the photograph and the picture on the TV screen. So is faith **the substance of things** that God has given us through His promises.

12
Being Fully Persuaded

David said:

The entrance of thy words giveth light; it giveth understanding unto the simple.

Psalm 119:130

Nearly 4,000 years before the Polaroid camera was invented, David had some understanding concerning polarization of light. God's Word will polarize your spirit. The entrance of the Word will enlighten and change your spirit to the point that you are fully persuaded, then you will draw the blessings promised like a magnet draws metal. (See Joshua 1:8.)

Abraham is a good example. He **against hope believed in hope, that he might become the father of many nations, according to that which was spoken** (Rom. 4:18).

Now the Lord had said unto Abram, Get thee out of thy country, and from thy kindred, and from thy father's house, unto a land that I will shew thee:

And I will make of thee a great nation, and I will bless thee, and make thy name great; and thou shalt be a blessing.

Genesis 12:1,2

Abraham was 75 years old at this time! (v. 4.) He had the promise, but 24 years later, he still didn't have the manifestation of that promise.

Later God came to him in a vision saying: **Fear not, Abram: I am thy shield, and thy exceeding great reward** (Gen. 15:1).

Genesis 15:2-5 states:

And Abram said, Lord GOD, what wilt thou give me, seeing I go childless, and the steward of my house is this Eliezer of Damascus?

And Abram said, Behold, to me thou hast given no seed: and, lo, one born in my house is mine heir.

And, behold, the word of the Lord came unto him, saying, This shall not be thine heir; but he that shall come forth out of thine own bowels shall be thine heir.

And he brought him forth abroad, and said, Look now toward heaven, and tell the stars, if thou be able to number them: and he said unto him, So shall thy seed be.

Notice what verse 2 above says. Abram asked God, "What will You give me seeing that I go childless?" That was Abram's image of himself — "I am childless." So God took him out and showed him the stars of heaven and said, "So shall thy seed be." The childless image had to be changed before the promise could be manifest.

Then we see in Genesis 17:4 God appeared to Abram again and said, **As for me, behold, my covenant is with thee, and thou shalt be a father of many nations.**

At this time Abraham was 99 years old! Abram had the promise for 24 years with no manifestation of it. He wasn't fully polarized with the light of God's Word. He wasn't yet fully persuaded at this point. Then God did something that would perfect that image forever.

Neither shall thy name any more be called Abram, but thy name shall be

Abraham; for a father of many nations
have I made thee.

Genesis 17:5

Remember that the entrance of God's words brings light, and faith in God comes by hearing the Word of God. (Ps. 119:130, Rom. 10:17.) God changed Abram's name to "Abraham" because Abraham means "father of many nations" (or "father of a multitude" — Gen. 17:5 AMP).

In other words God said, "As far as I am concerned, I have already made you a father of nations." He was saying, "My word is out, so I've already done it."

As far as God was concerned, the whole thing was settled back there 24 years before — but it wasn't fully settled with Abraham, for he had an image of being childless. God knew when He changed His name, it would eventually change Abram's image, and he would be fully persuaded.

Every time Abraham said, "My name is 'Abraham,'" everyone knew what that name implied. He didn't have to tell them that it meant "father of many nations." In those days they knew what names meant.

Every time someone called Abraham's name, he didn't just hear his name — he heard "father of nations." God forced Abram to say what He had said about him by the name change. The light of God's Word eliminated the image of being childless. The intense light from speaking God's words after him polarized Abraham's spirit, and he became fully persuaded.

Romans 4:18 says of Abraham:

> **Who against hope believed in hope, that he might become the father of many nations, according to that which was spoken, So shall thy seed be.**

When there was no hope, Abraham believed in hope. The doctors may have told you, "There's no hope for you physically." Your accountant may have told you, "There's no hope for you financially." Do as Abram did; go to God's Word and get some supernatural hope. Get your spirit polarized and charged with God's Word. Then you won't have to proofread the copy.

Less than a year after God changed Abraham's name, the promised child was born. That is not a coincidence! Abraham became fully persuaded.

Romans 4:19-22 says:

> And being not weak in faith, he considered not his own body now dead, when he was about an hundred years old, neither yet the deadness of Sarah's womb:

> He staggered not at the promise of God through unbelief; but was strong in faith, giving glory to God;

> And being fully persuaded that, what he had promised, he was able also to perform.

> And therefore it was imputed to him for righteousness.

For 24 years he had the promise, but it didn't come to pass until Abraham started saying what God said about him: "The word is nigh Abram in his mouth and in his heart — that is, the word of faith that Abram spoke to become fully persuaded." (Rom. 10:8.)

13

The Parable
of the Seed

I was teaching a seminar at the Russellville Christian Center in June 1988 in Russellville, Arkansas. Before the service that night, the Lord gave me a psalm. It was actually a synopsis of what I was teaching that night. I called it "The Parable of the Seed."

When the seed is sown in the earth, before the sun can rise and set, the seed has demanded that your need be met. The heart will respond without regret, but the process has only begun, and it is not revealed yet.

But have confidence and respect for the seed, for it has given its life for what you need.

It will work night and day giving substance to what you say. It will assemble the information piece by piece and know the exact time for its release.

So set a watch on what you speak and how you pray, for a time of release comes every day. Take heed to the words that God has spoken and obey, for you see the fruit is being fashioned each day.

The process continues until the harvest is perfected in this very way, for day after day the seed demands and the earth does obey, but be careful not to tamper with the seed, for if you do, you may come up with a weed.

But if you will encourage it with the water of the Word, it will supply your every need.

Jesus said:

Except a corn of wheat fall into the ground and die, it abideth alone: but if it die, it bringeth forth much fruit.

John 12:24

That seed gives its life for what you need, and that's exactly what Jesus did.

He gave His life for what you need. When God wanted righteousness in the earth, He planted His Seed. Jesus was the Seed of righteousness. He gave His life so that you might become the righteousness of God in Him.

When you accept Jesus Christ as your Savior, you become the righteousness of God in Christ. Even though you may not look righteous; you might not even act righteous at times, but be diligent to proclaim what God's Word has said about you. Get in agreement with Him and decree it until light comes.

When the light of God's Word, has infused His image into your spirit, you will not struggle with fear or faith, for you you are fully persuaded; you possess the substance of things.

Charles Capps is a former farmer and land developer who travels throughout the United States, teaching and preaching God's Word. He shares from practical, first-hand experience how Christians can apply the Word to the circumstances of life and live victoriously.

Besides authoring several books, including the best-selling *The Tongue, A Creative Force*, Charles also has a nationwide radio ministry called "Concepts of Faith."

Charles and his wife Peggy make their home in England, Arkansas. Both their daughters, Annette and Beverly, are involved in the ministry.

OTHER BOOKS BY CHARLES CAPPS

For additional copies
of this book
in Canada contact:

Word Alive
P. O. Box 670
Niverville, Manitoba
CANADA R0A 1EO

The Harrison House Vision

Proclaiming the truth and the power
Of the Gospel of Jesus Christ
With excellence;

Challenging Christians to
Live victoriously,
Grow spiritually,
Know God intimately